A Note to Parents

DK READERS is a compelling program for beginning readers, designed in conjunction with leading literacy experts, including Dr. Linda Gambrell, Distinguished Professor of Education at Clemson University. Dr. Gambrell has served as President of the National Reading Conference, the College Reading Association, and the International Reading Association.

Beautiful illustrations and superb full-color photographs combine with engaging, easy-to-read stories to offer a fresh approach to each subject in the series. Each DK READER is guaranteed to capture a child's interest while developing his or her reading skills, general knowledge, and love of reading.

The five levels of DK READERS are aimed at different reading abilities, enabling you to choose the books that are exactly right for your child:

Pre-level 1: Learning to read
Level 1: Beginning to read
Level 2: Beginning to read alone
Level 3: Reading alone
Level 4: Proficient readers

The "normal" age at which a child begins to read can be anywhere from three to eight years old. Adult participation through the lower levels is very helpful for providing encouragement, discussing storylines, and sounding out unfamiliar words.

No matter which level you select, you can be sure that you are helping your child learn to read, then read to learn!

LONDON, NEW YORK, MUNICH,
MELBOURNE, and DELHI

In memory of Joanne Olive Murphy

Series Editor Deborah Lock
U.S. Editor John Searcy
Managing Art Editor Rachael Foster
Art Editor Chris Hamilton-Brown
Production Editor Sean Daly
Production Erika Pepe
Illustrator Peter Dennis
Map Illustrator Ed Merritt

Subject Consultant Pamela Petterson,
Information Specialist (retired),
National Historic Oregon Trail
Interpretive Center

Reading Consultant
Linda Gambrell, Ph.D.

First American Edition, 2008
08 09 10 11 12 10 9 8 7 6 5 4 3 2 1
Published in the United States by DK Publishing
375 Hudson Street, New York, New York 10014

DK books are available at special discounts when purchased
in bulk for sales promotions, premiums,
fund-raising, or educational use.
For details, contact: DK Publishing Special Markets
375 Hudson Street, New York, New York 10014
SpecialSales@dk.com

A catalog record for this book is available
from the Library of Congress
ISBN: 978-0-7566-4005-7 (Paperback)
ISBN: 978-0-7566-4004-0 (Hardcover)

Color reproduction by MDP, UK
Printed and bound in China by L. Rex Printing Co. Ltd.

The publisher would like to thank the following for their kind
permission to reproduce their photographs:
(Key: a=above; b=below/bottom; c=center; l=left; r=right; t=top)
Alamy Images: John Elk III 32cla, 32tr; Chuck Haney / Danita
Delimont 29tr; Mark Newman / Agency Photo Network 22; Bob
Pardue 15tr; Visual Arts Library (London) 11. **Corbis:** James L.
Amos 27br. **Getty Images:** MPI / Hulton Archive 12. **L.Tom Perry
Special Collections, Harold B. Lee Library, Brigham Young
University, Provo, Utah:** 31tr. **Le Ti Coin Creole - Grill and
Seafood Restaurant:** 32br. **Mary Evans Picture Library:** 25t. **The
Oregon Trail / Boettcher / Trinklein Inc.:** 13tr. **StockFood.com:**
Foodfolio 24crb. **Wikipedia, The Free Encyclopedia:** 16br.
All other images © Dorling Kindersley
For more information see: www.dkimages.com

Discover more at
www.dk.com

DK READERS

BEGINNING TO READ ALONE 2

Journey of a Pioneer

Written by Patricia J. Murphy

DK Publishing

Dear Diary,

My name is Olivia Clark and I've lived in Elk Grove, Missouri, my whole life. But that's about to change.

Pa heard that many farming
families are moving west to
Oregon Territory.
They're looking for free,
open land and a new start.
Since times are tough and our
little plot of land can't produce
many crops, we're leaving, too.
Pa told us at supper.
I can't sleep.

Ma said Oregon Territory is far away and it will take many months to get there. Pa warned that we'd travel long distances through wilderness. Sometimes we'll be the only white folks around!

The Oregon Trail was a 2,000-mile (3,200 km) path from Missouri to Oregon Territory, passing natural landmarks and crossing rivers. It was used from 1843 to the 1870s.

Oregon City
The Dalles
OREGON TERRITORY
Flagstaff Hill
Three Island Crossing
Snake River
Soda Springs
South Pass
Chimne Roc
MEXICAN TERRITORY
Independence Rock
Scotts Bluff

Once we arrive, we'll have a very
large plot of land all to ourselves.
This means a bigger house,
a barn for the animals,
and space to grow lots of crops.
I hope I like it there,
wherever *there* is.

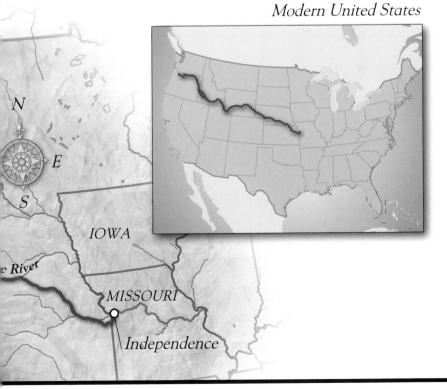

Modern United States

N

E

S

IOWA

e River

MISSOURI

Independence

We've been selling our furniture and anything else that won't fit in our wagon. Ma has filled large barrels with food and packed our cooking tools, china, and bedding into a trunk.

I've packed my doll, Johanna,
but will leave her bed behind.
Pa said that he would build
Johanna another bed when
he makes our new furniture.
He has bought oxen to pull
the wagon.

Today, we said our last goodbyes. Grandma hugged me so tight I almost stopped breathing.

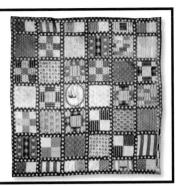

Ma cried when friends gave her
a friendship quilt.
Pa had tears in his eyes, too.
I wondered why everyone was
so sad.
Ma told me later that we might
not see many of these people
ever again.
I didn't want to believe her,
but Ma never lies.

May 4, 1845 Today, we reached our "jumping off" point—Independence, Missouri. We bought last-minute wagon supplies here and met up with others heading west.

Wagons gathering in Independence, Missouri

First traffic jams
With hundreds of
wagons heading west
at one time, slower-
moving wagons caused
long stretches of traffic.

We've split up into groups of
wagons called "trains."
Each train includes men with
important skills, such as doctors,
blacksmiths, and builders.
In our train, there is
also a girl
named Lizzie.
She could be
my new best friend.

We've settled into a daily routine now.
We wake as the sun rises.
Ma makes breakfast.
Pa hitches up the oxen.
We pack up our things
and away we go.

Independence Rock

To avoid traveling in the winter, families hoped to get to Independence Rock, Wyoming, by the Fourth of July.

Most of the day, we walk behind the wagon.

Sometimes, we pick wildflowers.

We travel up to 15 miles (24 km) until night falls—or we fall over.

We "make camp" when we find a spot with enough grass and water for the oxen.

Pa unhitches the oxen and lets them rest.

I collect dead sagebrush and dried buffalo dung for the fire and help put up our tent.

Ma makes dinner.

Forming a corral

Each night, the travelers put their wagons in a circle to keep their animals in and wild animals out.

Tonight, we used a tablecloth and candles since it was Pa's birthday. For a minute, it felt a little like home.

After dinner, we clear the table, wash dishes, and make beds in the tent. On special nights, Pa and others play their fiddles and harmonicas. We sing and dance under the moon.

Most nights, we just want to rest.
I count backward to get to sleep.
It keeps me from wondering how
close the howling animals are.
Men take turns "sitting watch"
to protect the camp.

July 7, 1845

I try to be brave when we cross rivers, but it can be cold, wet, and scary. When the rivers are low, we just walk across. When the rivers are high, we wait until they are lower, and then the oxen pull the wagons across.

As we cross, we watch
the fast-moving river currents.
Yesterday, one man drowned
and two wagons tipped over.
The families lost everything.

*Wagons were sealed
with tar or pitch
to prevent leaks.*

July 28, 1845   I have seen Indians from far away a few times, but today I saw my first Indian up close. He was tall, thin, and had dark hair and skin. He wore leather and feathers. He offered us buffalo meat. Ma gave him some blankets in return.

Buffalo stampede
Travelers had more to fear from buffalo than from Indians. A stampede could trample them to death.

Pa traded some nails and beads
for some moccasins.
Indians aren't as scary as
I thought they would be.

August 3, 1845 Meals on the trail are different than they were back home. Most days, we eat cornmeal, beans, or rice, served with bacon or dried beef. On windy or rainy days, we can't start fires, so everyone has cold meals.

Coarse cornmeal

Dried beef

Rice

Cornmeal porridge

If Pa goes hunting, he might
bring back an antelope or catch
a rabbit or a bird for us to eat.
When we find berries,
Ma uses them to make
fresh-baked pies.

Blackberries

Elderberries

August 9, 1845 After endless prairies, we've finally reached the mountains, but climbing the steep sides is hard work! To go up, we have to lighten our load, which means dumping Ma's stove and trunk.

To get down, we tie rope to a tree and then the back of the wagon. Then we slowly let out the rope. The Rocky Mountains are too steep. Luckily, we used a flat, wide path through them called South Pass. Oregon Territory is close!

Oregon City

OREGON TERRITORY

South Pass

South Pass

South Pass was a 12-mile (19 km) wide trail through the otherwise impassable Rocky Mountains.

August 18, 1845 On the trail, we have seen births, celebrated holidays, and marked many special events.
We have seen tragedy, too. Some people have become very ill and died.

Others have been struck by
lightning, shot while hunting,
drowned in river crossings, and
killed by wagons and buffalo.
The trail is filled with goodbyes.
Today, Lizzie and her family
set off on another path
to a different part of
Oregon Territory.
I will miss her.

September 28, 1845 After 2,000 miles (3,200 km) and five months of traveling, we've arrived in Willamette Valley, Oregon Territory. After a few days rest, we picked the plot of land where we'll live and farm. Once we've built our house, we'll have a big celebration with eating and dancing. We'll celebrate the end of our long journey and the beginning of our new life in Oregon Territory—our new home!

Pioneer diaries

Historians believe that
one in every 250 pioneers
kept diaries or journals
along the trail, recording
their risky journey.

Pioneer facts

In 1805, Meriwether Lewis and William Clark were the first explorers from the United States to reach Oregon Territory. Other explorers, fur trappers, church people, and settlers followed afterward, finding better routes from the east to the west coasts of America.

About 200,000 pioneers traveled west along the Oregon Trail. At first, people used maps and guides to find their way. Later on, they just followed the well-worn ruts from the earlier pioneers' wagon wheels.

Pioneers were called "emigrants." This was because the Oregon Territory was not yet part of the United States. An emigrant is someone who leaves one country and settles in another.

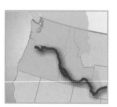

Oregon Territory was later divided into the states of Oregon, Washington, Idaho, small parts of Wyoming and Montana, as well as much of British Columbia, Canada.

Pioneers had fast food, too! Many pioneers' favorite food was the johnnycake, which was like a fluffy pancake. Pioneers could fold them and put them in their pockets until they were ready to eat them.